GBN Global Business Network
a member of the Monitor Group

LEARNINGS from the
Long View

Peter Schwartz
COFOUNDER, GLOBAL BUSINESS NETWORK

CONTENTS

INTRODUCTION

The Art of the Long View was first published in 1991. Nearly two decades later, it sells thousands of copies each year, many to prospective MBAs. It is required reading at business schools from Harvard to Kellogg to Wharton. By far the best-known book on constructing scenarios, it helped pave the way for the widespread adoption of scenario planning methods in the corporate world and beyond.

Yet when I wrote the book in 1990, I had a relatively limited set of experiences to draw on. Most of my knowledge about foresight and scenario planning was drawn from my previous workplaces, Royal Dutch Shell and the Stanford Research Institute. The company I cofounded and covered in the book—Global Business Network (GBN)—was a mere three years old.

After almost 25 years, GBN has an extraordinarily rich legacy. We've done hundreds of projects with hundreds of clients. We have worked with dozens of Fortune 500 companies as well as nonprofits, NGOs, and governmental groups, large and small, around the world. We have collected one or two anecdotes along the way.

So this little book has several purposes. First, I will share what I have learned at GBN since 1990—mistakes as well as successes. I'll also take stock of the original *Art of the Long View*, noting what I got right (the rise of the global teenager, empowered by new technology; the two out of three scenarios that accurately depicted our world in the last two decades) as well as what I got wrong (my chapter on where to hunt for information, for example, which didn't mention the nascent Web). Finally, I'll plunge forward once more—looking at the next great global driving force (hint: it's a lot more troubling than teenagers), and constructing three scenarios for the year 2025.

What follows, then, is a memoir, a mea culpa, and a map of the future.

LEARNING FROM OUR MISTAKES

Though scenario planning is one of the best ways to prepare for an uncertain future, it is by no means infallible. Peering at what's next is invariably a risky proposition. Over the years, GBN and I, personally, have been blindsided on a number of occasions. I'd like to share four important mistakes that have been instructive. They deal with the invasion of Kuwait by Iraq in 1990, the Mexican peso crisis of 1994, the destructive mindset of a client CEO, and the recent devastating financial crisis.

Bad Call 1: Kuwait

On the evening of August 1, 1990, I was on my way to have dinner in Chicago with Bob Darnall, the CEO of Inland Steel. The steel industry was going through some major structural changes at the time. We were preparing for a presentation for his board the next day that looked at the future landscape of the business, one that covered everything from energy costs to the state of the competition.

When I arrived for dinner, Bob was a little concerned about something he'd just heard on the radio. Apparently, Iraq's army was massing on the border with Kuwait. Was this important? Should he be worried about it? Would it affect the presentation? Energy — for making steel and transporting it — was one of the company's largest overhead costs. If there was a war in the Middle East, the price of oil would spike. Not only that, an invasion would have a serious effect on economic growth, which is closely related to the demand for steel. It could be a disaster for Inland.

I chewed it over for about three nanoseconds. Then I said, "No Bob, I really wouldn't worry too much about this. I think it's mostly bluff."

I was basing this answer on my experience of the oil trading business in the mid-1980s, during the Iran-Iraq War. In those days, when Iraq needed to renegotiate big contracts, they would bomb a refinery or a tanker to firm up the market. Saddam Hussein had a history of using military action in support of his trading strategies.

By the time of our meeting with the board the following morning, Saddam had completed his invasion of Kuwait, and the United States was heading toward war. It had been no bluff, but a major global crisis in the making.

I looked like an idiot, to say the least. Fortunately, my bad advice did not cause Inland any trouble. I was proven wrong so fast that they didn't have to change direction as a result. At the board meeting Bob, mercifully, didn't give me too much grief for my error the night before. And I was able to pivot and turn it into a learning experience for Bob and the board. This, I said, is why you should spend some time constructing and preparing for multiple scenarios. No one expert can give you a simple guide to the future.

Having said that, what was my mistake? It was forgetting my own advice—the advice I put at the center of *The Art of the Long View*. I wasn't challenging my mental maps. My instincts told me to use a concept from the world of oil trading five years previously. Indeed, there had been a longstanding issue between Iraq and Kuwait over an oil field that spanned their borders: who had access to it and who could sell the oil from it. I used that knowledge to make a rapid judgment.

Now, rapid judgments aren't always wrong, and there is a certain class of problems for which they work very well. I don't entirely disagree with the theory about rapid judgment put forward in Malcolm Gladwell's bestseller *Blink*. That, in fact, is how a good scenario is born—it's a very intuitive process. The trouble is that if you have only one scenario for the future of your company—as I had come up with one quick scenario that night—the consequences are enormous. That's why you have to keep looking at the questions from different angles. My colleagues at GBN often challenge my perceptions and lead me to think and ask better questions, but I didn't have any around me that night.

Lesson 1: We are all prone to leaping to easy conclusions. I did not follow my own process of considering other scenarios or different interpretations of the situation. In a complex, uncertain situation, even a scenario planner is vulnerable to an instantaneous judgment and forecast. It is always worth asking yourself: "how could I be wrong?"

Bad Call 2: Mexico

Of course, even a whole mass of experts following standard scenario-creation practices can be blindsided. That's what happened during the Mexican peso crisis of 1994.

Throughout the 1990s, GBN had a membership service called WorldView. It was a network of 50–80 companies in virtually every industry that we connected to our network of 100 visionary thinkers—our "remarkable people" or RPs. One of the ways we did that was by hosting meetings to bring these people together in an extended and informed conversation on various themes and trends of emerging importance. We held these meetings all around the world—from the Biosphere in Arizona to a former prison in Sweden to Hong Kong as it prepared to rejoin China.

In December 1994 we met at a resort just outside of Mexico City. The subject, not surprisingly, was the future of Mexico. It was a time of great optimism in the country. That month saw a change of president from Carlos Salinas to Ernesto Zedillo, who had won a landslide victory. Salinas had been the first of the country's technocratic presidents. He had been seen as moving Mexico in the right direction. But Zedillo, a former economist and secretary of education, was going to be a real shot in the arm for progress and modernization. We felt he was going to clean up corruption even more than Salinas had.

There were other reasons for optimism. The North American Free Trade Agreement (NAFTA) had just come into effect that year, eliminating most

trade tariffs. The relationship between Mexico and the U.S. was open-
ing up, and the interconnection between the two countries seemed to be
deeper than ever. Mexico looked set for an economic takeoff. It had low
inflation and a small budget surplus. There was a rapidly growing and
youthful population in the cities, more open trade, and signs that the
state appeared to be modernizing. All these driving forces seemed to point
to a bright future. Was that inevitable? Were there other scenarios? That's
what we intended to find out.

So as Salinas was leaving office and Zedillo was coming into power, we
gathered together more than 30 of our member organizations, a few of our
RPs, and a group of Mexican business leaders, economists, and thinkers.
They all helped inform our conversation about the future of Mexico. Over
the course of two days we discussed a variety of possibilities and laid out
a grand total of eight scenarios for how the country might develop.

The outcome of those scenarios ranged from fair to good to very good. In
the first round of scenario planning, the Mexico experts' greatest fear was
that Zedillo might be assassinated before the end of his term. The second round of scenarios dealt more explicitly with economic matters. Two
scenarios saw Mexico evolving into an economic powerhouse, in much
the same way as China has developed. The worst-case scenario was called
"Return to Underdevelopment," in which Mexico's growth was hampered
by a rise in union power. The scenarios seemed to span a variety of possibilities and different interpretations of the capacity of the new government and the impact of NAFTA. They all seemed plausible and realistic.

Two weeks after our meeting, the Mexican peso completely collapsed.

Before the election, Salinas had kept the peso at a fixed rate, even though
Mexico had borrowed a massive amount of money. It was not uncommon
for this to happen, or for the incoming president to devalue the currency.
Zedillo had promised not to do this. But indeed, shortly after his election
he let it float, with disastrous results.

In the space of a week, the exchange rate went from four pesos per dollar to more than seven pesos per dollar. The market's uncertainty had exploded. The survival of Mexico's entire economy seemed in doubt. And there had not been for a moment any indication in our scenarios that this event was possible in the near future, let alone the long term.

The crisis was resolved with what amounted to a $50 billion international bailout. Some $20 billion of that came from the U.S. That may not seem like much in our post-financial crisis world, but it was seen as a large sum at the time. President Clinton had to do an end run around critics in Congress and offer the loans through a Treasury program.

Thanks to NAFTA, the two countries were tied together as closely as if Mexico were the fifty-first state. The U.S. had to take action in a timely way to keep Mexico from going bankrupt. It succeeded — Mexico paid the money back by the end of the decade, faster than expected, and the U.S. made $500 million in interest.

Still, the crisis had a profound impact on Mexican development. Zedillo was unable to accomplish much of his agenda. NAFTA didn't get off to a great start. Many observers in the U.S. became uneasy that NAFTA had so intimately connected the two countries that we had to rescue them or they would have pulled us into a financial vortex. It was a classic case of an economy that was "too big to fail."

So the scenarios we had developed were completely off the mark, to say the least. We entirely missed a crisis that was not in the distant future, but was imminent. Worse, its precursors were already evident. Devaluation had happened after many previous elections in Mexico, even if the consequences weren't always this large.

How did we get it so wrong? The answer was something we only realized in hindsight: we had an inadequate diversity of views. Our participants were part of the same intellectual community, engaged in the same conversation, both in Mexico and outside. By and large, they had agreed on an "Official Future" — another mistake I had cautioned against in *The Art of the Long View.* They were not seeing many of the forces at work in the Mexican economy, even though we knew that Mexico tended to go through some kind of financial crisis every time the presidency changed. We talked about it and said, "Well, now they've finally gotten it under control. This time is different." By being in denial about historical precedent, we set our narrow views in stone.

We see this time and time again in world events. "This time is different" was a common refrain during the recent real estate bubble. It's something we hear a lot when dynamic new leaders are elected, not just Zedillo. How often are we wrong?

Lesson 2: Diversity really does matter. Inviting people into the conversation who make you uncomfortable is a very good idea. Sometimes they're awkward. Sometimes they can't make their case very well. But they can be very important to the process. And if an event has happened multiple times in the history of your subject, you need to a) explain why it wouldn't happen again (which we did), and b) examine how it could happen again (which we didn't). Devising too narrow a range of scenarios is almost as dangerous as holding to an Official Future.

Bad Call 3: The Mining Company

Perhaps the most painful lesson in GBN's history came about during a project with a major mining company in 1992. This company was in the business of mining, refining, and selling a precious metal. Its profits were entirely dependent on the price of the commodity and the cost of its production. The company's view of the future price of the commodity shaped its strategy. The market had seen some very large movements in the price of that precious metal — from all-time highs a decade previously to roughly half that price in the early 1990s.

The CEO had embarked on a major program of acquisitions. The first phase of this plan was relatively low-cost and uncontroversial. But increasingly, he was buying companies around the world where the cost was high and the currency risks were amplified, as were the political risks. He got into bidding wars with other major mining companies. Every time a new acquisition was brought before the board, the CEO insisted that the price of the precious metal was going to rise fairly soon and make all of these acquisitions highly profitable.

We were brought in by the CFO of another client of ours, with whom we had a very good relationship. He was on the board of the mining company, and was concerned that the CEO was betting the farm on his Official Future. So, at the request of the board, the CEO agreed to do a scenario project with us to look at the future dynamics of pricing.

We led the CEO and about a dozen of his top staff through an exercise that came up with a total of five scenarios, each of which were seen as quite plausible. There were a couple of scenarios where the price of the precious metal would remain low for quite a long time and the company would lose money for a number of years. Maybe the acquisitions would prove their worth someday, but that would take a lot longer than the CEO was expecting. There were a couple of scenarios in which the price went up—the precious metal was useful in the booming computer industry, for one thing—and the acquisitions would look very good very soon. And there was a scenario in which the price was highly volatile. The obvious conclusion was that when it came to pricing, there was a wide range of uncertainty. We finished the project, presented the results, and left thinking that we had served our client well.

A few weeks later, we discovered to our horror that almost half the participants in the workshop had been fired. Heads of finance, technology, and operations were all gone. The CEO, it turned out, had not taken the scenario process as a learning experience—at least, not the one we intended. He had spent his time at the workshop finding out who disagreed with his favored scenario so he could get rid of them. His argument was that he needed a team that agreed with his strategy, since he was going to drive the company hard in that direction. The fired executives were betrayed. So were we.

In the consulting business, as in the medical trade, we take seriously the words of the Hippocratic Oath: "First, do no harm." Sometimes projects don't work out. Sometimes GBN is not all that helpful. (Most of the time we are, of course, otherwise we wouldn't have survived in business this long.) But this was the one case where we actually did harm. Our tools were misused, and did great damage to people's lives.

The failure, ultimately, was ours: we had failed to understand the psychology of the CEO. He was a hardscrabble mining engineer who'd come up from the roots of the trade. He had a reputation for being ruthless. He was driven so hard to succeed that he was quite capable of convincing himself that he was right, no matter what. In his mind, anybody who didn't see things his way was a great risk to the company. He had no trouble justifying the firing of dissenters, no matter if it was based on an exercise where his people were supposed to be thinking and talking freely.

What did we do? In short, we fired the client. We gave the money back for the project. But there was little we could do to repair the harm. With hindsight, I think we had not dug deeply enough into the CEO's psychology or the culture of this organization, which he had run for a long time. Had we known about his ruthless reputation, we might have exercised greater caution in what we did and how we did it.

What happened to the mining company? The CEO had enough allies on the board that he clung to his position. The precious metal remained cheap for many years. Still, the CEO persisted with buying smaller companies. One acquisition in particular almost bankrupted the company. After that, the board fired the CEO. But it was too late: the company was bleeding money, and was ultimately acquired by its largest competitor.

Ironically, the price of the precious metal spiked in the mid-2000s. Had the CEO been less aggressive in his acquisitions, his company would have survived and his faith in the markets would have been rewarded. The last I heard of him, he was running a far smaller mining operation in the West.

Lesson 3: Scenarios aren't just about the intellectual challenge. They're about the people around the table. You need to create a safe space for the free flow of ideas. If someone in a position of power has been brought into the room unwillingly, and/or believes strongly in an Official Future, that should set alarm bells ringing.

Bad Call Four: The Financial Crisis

It was almost a given that the 2000s would see some kind of financial crisis. In my 2003 book *Inevitable Surprises* and in many scenario presentations over the last 10 years, I noted that every decade has its major market meltdown, regardless of how rosy the outlook seems. Even the 1990s, the most sustained period of economic growth the U.S. has ever seen, was not immune. The last such crisis was 1997 in Southeast Asia, caused by the government of Thailand, which had taken on a massive amount of foreign debt and devalued its currency. It was highly consequential in that part of the world, but it managed to avoid becoming a global crisis (thanks largely to the swift intervention of the IMF). Russia had its own brief financial wobble a year later, also prompted by a currency crisis.

In a set of scenarios GBN developed for the country of Singapore, we saw the likelihood of major financial crises in the U.S. or China and pointed to the banking system as the potential source. Peter Ho, the permanent secretary of the foreign ministry and chief of the civil service, initiated the study. In late 2007, Ho had become concerned that the world was heading toward a major fiscal breakdown and asked us to look at the scenarios that could develop. We presented the results to the leadership of Singapore in the spring of 2008.

The scenarios covered a wide range of outcomes from a rapid recovery to an extended recession and delayed recovery all the way to a renewed and deeper crisis. The course that events took most closely resembled the second scenario. The analysis behind it was revealing, and became quite influential in Singapore's key ministries. The country weathered the economic storm rather well. In the second quarter of 2010, Singapore's export market grew by 26 percent. In that sense, we got it right.

What we had missed completely was the magnitude of the crisis.

The first thing we failed to see was how interconnected the global banking system had become. More and more debt got securitized, and those securities were distributed through a great variety of financial institutions, creating a complex set of portfolios for clients all over the world. Suddenly, foreclosures in St. Louis ended up bankrupting small communities in Germany whose funds were in banks that had invested in other funds, which had invested in other funds, which owned those bad mortgages. The nation of Iceland had been a large part of this global securitization process, generating great returns for its banking customers — until short-term lending seized up. Iceland lost its ability to borrow money, it had to devalue its currency, and three of its major banks collapsed.

The second thing we failed to see was the sheer size of what amounted to a shadow economy. Banks were generating enormous profits from selling and trading complex instruments such as derivatives and collateralized debt obligations (CDOs). But the instruments themselves were off the balance sheets of the banks, so few people knew how much money had been pumped into them. The amount turned out to be roughly 10 times what most analysts thought.

I remember one conversation that brought this fact into sharp relief. In November 2008, I was on my way to a World Economic Forum meeting in Dubai, sharing a limo with William White, the chief economist of the Bank of International Settlements (BIS). The BIS sets the standard for how much cash a bank must have to cover the amount of debt it issues. If anyone on the planet should have known the banks' true balance sheets, it was White. But when we started to discuss the financial crisis, White said that none of the banks had reported their off-the-books debt to him. They weren't required to. Furthermore, he added, it was probably an order of magnitude larger than anything he would have ever imagined.

So could we have foreseen the magnitude of the crisis when creating those financial scenarios? I believe we could have, if we'd dug deeply enough. When we considered potential crises, we thought the effects were likely to be significant but containable. We believed that institutions such as the Fed and the International Monetary Fund and BIS had learned how to manage these matters effectively. We thought we didn't need to be too worried, having weathered the crises we experienced in the 1990s. It was the Official Future for the financial world.

If we had asked the right questions of people like White earlier, we might have discovered how large the shadow economy was and how everyone's debt was interconnected. We might have gone looking for naysayers such as the economist Nouriel Roubini, who warned Wall Street about the housing bubble as early as 2005. He saw the dangerous interconnections of these new debt instruments sooner than most. I knew of Roubini's position, and took it seriously, but also considered him something of an outlier. A debt implosion scenario might be bad, I figured, but it probably wouldn't be that bad. (As it turned out, not even Roubini knew just how much debt was floating around the shadow economy).

Lesson 4: When creating scenarios, always ask the questions: Could your data be wrong? Could potential problems be bigger than anyone thinks? How can I challenge my deepest assumptions? In *The Art of the Long View*, I cautioned against developing apocalyptic scenarios, and I still think that holds true. But you can step up to the very brink of disaster, much as the world did in October 2008, and ask how you would respond to a crisis that is much bigger than the system can handle.

LEARNING FROM OUR SUCCESS

The last two decades have also seen plenty of times when our scenarios were particularly prescient, succeeded in changing the conversation, or influenced the entire strategy of a company. There are three examples I want to talk about: an early vision of the rise of the Internet, a new take on climate change that rocked the Pentagon, and a set of scenarios that led one of the world's largest oil companies to merge with a competitor.

Success Story 1:
Electronic Advertising and the "Interconnect"

In 1992, five large companies came to GBN to sponsor a project on the future of electronic advertising. They included a TV network, a film and TV studio, an international ad agency, and one of the world's leading consumer products companies. These companies all depended on TV ads for their livelihood and wanted to know how new technology would alter the advertising landscape. The fifth company was a regional telephone provider, which was starting to see the transformation of phone networks into a new form of distribution. What kind of advertising opportunities would that medium present?

It's important to remember that this was a time before DVDs, before TiVo, before the Web as we know it today. The Internet existed, but largely as an academic oddity. Few people had heard of it. Even those of us who were familiar with dial-up Internet services such as the Whole Earth 'Lectronic Link (WELL), founded by my friend and colleague Stewart Brand, didn't fully expect its usage to explode in the way it did. The first major web browser, Mosaic, hadn't been released. Satellite TV had yet to gain much of a foothold in the U.S. (the launch of DirecTV was still two years away). Nobody had even started to experiment with video on demand. Cable channels were all analog. These clients' greatest single concern at the time was the VCR—and the fact that consumers were manually fast-forwarding through the ads.

The scenario project, led ably by my colleague Lawrence Wilkinson, conjured up four visions of the year 2006. The first saw a crowded media landscape with a multiplicity of cable channels. In the second, a decline in the number of channels was matched by a boom in new kinds of home videos and videogames for the wealthiest Americans. The third saw electronic advertising and content shift away from the media at large and into retail stores. On the whole, these were fairly conservative scenarios. They preserved a great deal of the value that the companies around the table had to offer.

But the fourth scenario was about the radical transformation that came along with something we called the Interconnect. By the 2000s, we reasoned, phone companies and cable companies would provide competing high-speed data services—multiple commercial layers on top of the Internet that would be connected to each other by 2006 (hence "Interconnect"). More than 50 percent of households would have broadband. Most TV programming would be available online at any time. HDTV would flourish. Users would play rich interactive games with friends and strangers on the network. Software would be available for free with ads attached, and some users would pay for ad-free versions. Cellular telephone companies would run voice and data services over the network. Many Americans would telecommute, and spend a large portion of their newfound leisure time "on-line," watching videos, listening to music, and chatting with friends.

For our clients in 1992, this was a really challenging scenario. It disrupted nearly everything about the advertising landscape they knew. It forced them to think in really novel ways. It made the other three scenarios look like wishful thinking. And of course, as things turned out, it was a spookily accurate picture of 2006. (If anything, it was a little conservative—the concept of competing networks declined along with AOL, while the U.S. actually reached 50 percent broadband penetration a year earlier, in 2005.)

The fact that the participants were so engaged by this scenario was more heartening for me than its accuracy. That's especially true because we had some of the most respected names in each industry sitting around the table, such as Bob Iger from ABC (now the CEO of Disney), Dick Lindheim from Universal Studios, and Josh McQueen, a rising star in the advertising world. This is fairly unusual for a scenario generation process, which takes days of intense meetings and is often delegated to more low-level executives. It helped that we had Stewart Brand there to envisage a future version of the WELL, and that Lawrence Wilkinson — our point man — was an MBA who knew a great deal about the economics of content distribution and had previously headed a studio that produced advertising and special effects. In short, there was enough specialist knowledge in the room to make our discussion of this potential future very convincing.

For many of the participants, this scenario was a watershed moment. Dick Lindheim came away from it a changed man. It significantly altered the way he pursued his career. The vision of an immersive online environment led him away from film and towards virtual reality. Today, he runs RL Leaders, a laboratory that develops high-definition simulations for the military using advanced computer techniques.

The more engaged the participants were — and the higher up they sat in their respective companies — the more likely they were to alter their strategy. The TV network soon pursued a successful merger. The advertising agency got an early jump on new media marketing. At the other end of the spectrum, unfortunately, was the phone company. Its representative at our meetings was three tiers down the chain of command from the CEO. Despite his best efforts, the company made no significant moves to prepare for the Internet boom — until it was upon them.

Success Lesson 1: In the scenario creation process, invariably one scenario is going to embody the maximum amount of potential change and disruption to your business. This "stretch" scenario should also provoke the most engaging discussion about strategic implications.

The team also matters. The higher up the corporate food chain your scenario creators are, the more effective the result is likely to be. Even if the scenarios are being developed at lower levels, it's critical to get buy-in from the decision makers, at the very least through interviews and briefings.

Success Story 2: Climate Change and the Pentagon

In 2003, GBN was commissioned by Andy Marshall at the Department of Defense to do a study on the implications of abrupt climate change in the next couple of decades. I convinced Andy that this time frame could see a level of environmental disaster with some major consequences around the world, and that this was worth exploring from a national security point of view.

Andy's official title is Director of the Office of Net Assessments, a position he has held since 1973. His job is to be ahead of the curve, where he can explore the kind of potential future threats that most of the DoD doesn't have time to think about. The Secretary of Defense and the Chairman of the Joint Chiefs of Staff will regularly dine with Andy to discuss long-term issues. He is viewed as something of a legend at the Pentagon, and is regularly cited by people in positions of power.

Every year, Andy would commission a number of these kinds of studies. In the two decades I've known him, he has asked GBN to look into such issues as new patterns of geopolitics after the collapse of the Soviet Union, the future of China, and the impact of information technology. So the climate change study was not seen as an exceptionally big deal, even though the Bush Administration that Andy then worked for was notoriously skeptical of global warming. From his perspective, this was just one of a number of exploratory studies conducted by his office that year. It was his job to think the unthinkable.

My goal, meanwhile, was to produce a report that would start a conversation about abrupt climate change in the defense and intelligence communities. I've been studying the subject since the 1970s, when I was involved in a study on climate change conducted by the Stanford Research Institute. As an engineering student, I'd done a lot of work on the dynamics of complex turbulent fluids, and I came to realize that a smooth and gradual change in climate was extremely unlikely. Large increases in temperature can cause major disruptions, and major disruptions around the globe have enormous implications for national security.

This was not a standard GBN assignment. We weren't being asked to produce a range of scenarios. The question Andy wanted us to answer was this: how bad could climate change get, if it does happen abruptly? So when my colleague Doug Randall and I began the project, with some help from Stewart Brand and a few others, we were presented with a problem. It is extremely difficult, if not impossible, to predict exactly how the climate will change as a result of global warming over the next couple of decades. Not even the world's top climatologists can do it with any confidence. The system is inherently chaotic. How could we tell a credible story of abrupt climate change, while avoiding the charge that we had plucked our numbers out of thin air?

So we decided to look back through history in search of a useful model for climate change that took place within the space of a decade or two. We found what we were looking for 8,200 years in the past. Known to climatologists as the 8.2 kiloyear event, this was when the climate of the northern hemisphere cooled rather rapidly in less than a decade, stayed cool, windy and dry for the better part of a century, then warmed again in less than a decade. This was an example of abrupt climate change, then an abrupt change back again. It was impossible to argue that this cannot happen; it did happen. And though scientists don't know exactly why it happened, they do know the event turned off the ocean currents that warmed a lot of the northern hemisphere — just as global warming threatens to reach a tipping point where it turns off the North Atlantic Gulf Stream.

We used all the data we could find about the 8.2 kiloyear event and applied it to the world between 2010 and 2020. That meant a temperature drop of six degrees in a decade, on average. How large an effect would this have on ecosystems, and the viability of societies dependent upon those ecosystems?

The answers we found were pretty terrifying. There would be droughts around the world (especially in Southeast Asia), Siberia-like conditions in Europe, and a rising level of megastorms. Europe would be fighting back an influx of refugees from both Africa and Scandinavia. Oil and gas supplies would be stretched to the breaking point by the rising cold. Tensions would mount along a lot of borders, even the ones closest to home. Canada might decide to hoard its hydroelectric power while the U.S. feels forced to close itself off completely to the south and stops letting the Colorado River flow into Mexico. And as we have seen so many times in human history, when there is a dispute over shrinking resources, war would be almost inevitable.

So the results we presented to Andy Marshall, after three or four months of study and interviews with climatologists, were meaningful and serious. The report was published internally in the Pentagon, along with our recommendation that more resources be devoted to predictive climate models, adaptive response teams, and measures to make sure agriculture would remain intact no matter what. But was internal publication enough to get the wheels moving on this? After all, dozens of papers were published inside the Pentagon each year. Doug, Stewart and I had become convinced that this kind of abrupt change scenario was a grave and urgent threat to national security, far greater than cyber attacks, and greater even than the looming shadow of terrorism. There had to be some way to make it stand out. It was time to go to the press.

A couple of months later, with Andy's support, we presented the study to *Fortune* magazine. *Fortune* called the Pentagon to confirm that they could publish. After getting permission, *Fortune* ran "The Pentagon's Weather Nightmare" as a feature in February 2004, giving it precious space on the magazine's cover. The article generated a modest amount of interest.

Then something rather bizarre happened. One of London's most prestigious newspapers, *The Guardian*, ran a story claiming that there was a secret, suppressed Pentagon report on climate change — one that supposedly said Britain was facing imminent doom. Of course, this was wrong on a number of counts. The report was hypothetical. We did not kill off Britain; we merely pointed out that without the Atlantic Gulf Stream, the U.K. and most of northern Europe would revert to a climate similar to that of the Russian steppes. And the report hadn't been suppressed. It had made the front cover of *Fortune*.

Nevertheless, other press and blogs around the world quickly picked up the *Guardian* story and ran with allegations of a suppressed report on a massive climatic disaster about to hit the northern hemisphere. We fielded dozens of calls and interview requests, including one from "60 Minutes." We told them all that this was not a secret, suppressed report, much less a "smoking gun" as some had claimed. We pointed out that it had been published in a major magazine. And we stressed that the report was not a prediction, but a speculative exploration of the nature of the dynamics of change, based on one historical event repeating itself. The Pentagon did its bit to help squash the story too, including allowing GBN and a number of organizations to post the original report on their websites. Within a week or so, the brouhaha died down.

But in the meantime, it had attracted sufficient attention that it became a major subject of discussion at the Pentagon. The idea sank in. Soon thereafter, a group of admirals at the Center for Naval Analysis came out with a study that reached similar conclusions. One after another, additional studies confirmed that relatively abrupt climate change could have major impacts on national security.

We had set out to put climate change on the national security agenda, and we succeeded. Today almost every significant study of climate change policy — public or private — cites ours in some way. Not only that, but the scenario helped inspire the 2004 Fox film "The Day After Tomorrow." I got a call from the director, Roland Emmerich, asking me to help. But since the film dramatizes its miniature Ice Age by having it arrive in a couple of days, rather than years, I felt it was questionable science and chose not to participate. Looking back, I feel the movie's allegory helped advance the climate change conversation, and that audiences understood the distinction between that story and the science.

If we had to do the scenario again, we would probably have made it more about warming than cooling. It is still true that the climate is a chaotic system that could tip in any direction when prodded by enough carbon dioxide in the atmosphere. But because CO_2 levels are now likely to reach 550 parts per million — higher than we feared in 2003 — few scientists think it likely that any part of the world will get the kind of sustained cooling seen in the 8.2 kiloyear event. It's not impossible, especially in a Gulf Stream-free northern Europe. It's just less likely.

Still, our report had the right effect. It made people think about what happens when change is so rapid that human systems have a hard time adapting. It's one thing to have a century to adapt; it's another thing to have two to three years to adapt. We can't afford to be in denial about this kind of challenge.

A coda: Since 2004, we have done a number of climate change scenarios focused on warming. For example, we looked at the future of an ice-free Arctic for the Arctic Council, a group of nations with shorelines in the Arctic seas. The emerging reality is that the ice pack in the Arctic is shrinking steadily. In the next decade or two, the sea is likely to be almost ice-free for some of the year. The scenarios focused on two critical uncertainties: the demand for resources under the Arctic Sea, and how effectively this council of countries could regulate the area. A world of great demand and weak governments could yield a new kind of Arctic gold rush, with possibilities for conflict and major environmental damage. Weak demand allows time to develop better methods of regulating the area. How perceptive are these scenarios, and how helpful to the key players? It'll be some time before we know, but sadly, it won't be too long.

Success Lesson 2: When an important idea needs to be taken seriously, engaging the media can help (with appropriate attention to confidentiality and attribution, of course). Even if the story spins out of control the way ours did, an erroneous report is quickly corrected in today's active and transparent media environment. The broader discussion can actually lead even more people back to the real source.

Success Story 3: Texaco Takes a New Direction

This story is not about one project, but an extended process of organizational learning built around scenario planning. In the early 1990s, GBN began working with the Natural Gas Group of Texaco, based in Dallas, on a variety of scenarios looking at the future of natural gas. (Founded in 1902, Texaco had become a global energy company with revenues exceeding $30 billion.) We worked very closely with the head of that business, whose success drew the attention of the senior management.

He attributed part of his success to the efforts of the scenario planning group, which had helped him to see the evolution of the business more clearly. The result: not only was he promoted, but the team, led by a natural gas planner named Drew Overpeck, was brought to the Texaco corporate center in White Plains, New York, and became the core of a new company-wide strategic management group (SMG).

We worked closely with this team over the next several years at the corporate center. They conducted a number of scenario projects: the future of the Caspian Sea region, which is estimated to have $12 trillion in oil reserves; the appropriate strategies for the Gorgon Field, a huge natural gas field in Australia; and similar projects. They trained a number of people in the company in scenario planning. And there was cross-fertilization as a variety of people moved between the SMG and Operations groups.

Our work soon caught the attention of the CEO of Texaco, Peter Bijur, and in 1997 we started working on some global scenarios to help him think about the future direction of the company. With the help of an international team of 30 employees, drawn from all areas of Texaco's business, we came up with three possible futures. In the first, Texaco's access to its lifeblood was cut off. More and more oil-rich countries figured out that they could run their oil fields with the help of innovative companies that did not need an ownership stake. The second scenario saw the rise of the middlemen — intelligent companies that figured out how to package and sell units of energy to consumers and businesses, no matter what the source. Texaco and its ilk would be reduced to the status of bulk suppliers. And in the third scenario, new kinds of technology quickly supplanted the internal combustion engine. Consumers started driving electric cars, hybrid cars, and hydrogen fuel cell cars that could also power their homes.

It's fair to say that Bijur was inspired by these scenarios. He described them as "remarkable" and used them as the centerpiece of a number of major speeches to energy groups. But it wasn't just talk. Bijur had come into office thinking that his aim was to help Texaco become one of the agents of the industry's transformation. Now the scenarios convinced him that he needed to transform the company in a radical and surprising way. With so many threats to its core business, Bijur decided, Texaco could no longer survive on its own.

Bijur believed there was going to be major consolidation in the oil industry, and that Texaco would end up merging with another one of the petroleum giants: Chevron, Exxon, Shell, or BP. Therefore his strategy was to be the driver of a merger, not the unsuspecting victim of a takeover. And that is exactly what happened in 2001, when Texaco merged with Chevron. Shareholders in particular were pleased with the result. The stock has performed well ever since, relative both to the market and to its oil company peers.

So the story of our work with Texaco is one of persistence. This was not a one-off, a case of "let's try scenario planning and see how it works." It was an extended process of development over the course of a decade. The organization learned. It took a tool that was working on the periphery into the very center of the company, gaining new capabilities and new worldviews. Ultimately, it helped the CEO make one of the most momentous decisions of his life.

Not everything worked perfectly. In the early days of its tenure at Texaco headquarters, the SMG group butted heads with the corporate economist, a highly influential figure who saw these upstarts as supplanting his role. But the scenario planning process continued to yield impressive results, and the economist eventually became a fan. It helped that the group's leadership had the dogged determination to drive its projects forward for an entire decade. Drew Overpeck, in particular, deserves a lot of the credit. He had a wonderfully practical intelligence and a combination of technical and managerial skills. And he understood the company well enough to know how to get this work widely disseminated within it.

Success Lesson 3: Scenario planning doesn't have to stop with one project; embedding this posture and process of thinking about the future yields the most powerful results. If you stick with scenario planning over a number of years, the scenarios will inform and inspire a much richer strategic conversation up the corporate ladder and across functional and business units. Choosing the right people to be involved also matters—a diverse mix of decision makers, provocateurs, and people with deep knowledge of the business and industry will bring to bear critical perspectives, experiences, and an ability to act. The impact is increased by bringing your scenario-planning team into the very center of the organization—while also teaching scenario planning skills as widely as possible.

OTHER LESSONS

Foresight Training

We've also learned in the past 20-plus years that it is possible, and desirable, to teach other organizations how to do scenario planning. Every year we run public training courses for individuals from a variety of sectors, industries, and geographies as well as in-house programs for private companies, for nonprofits, and for governments. We have probably done this a dozen times a year for the last 15 years. That's well over 100 courses. Our students have included government agencies like the Department of Defense, the National Parks Service, and the EPA. In the United States we've taught companies such as Arco, Duke Power, Ford, Morgan Stanley, NBC Universal, and PG&E. Internationally, we have run the course for ABB, Fujitsu, Nissan, SingTel and Volvo, among many others.

But we didn't have scenario training figured out on Day One. Indeed, for many years, there was enormous debate within GBN about whether we should train others in a process that was, in many ways, our secret sauce. How could we develop a long-term relationship with clients like Texaco if we taught them how to develop scenarios without us? Some of my colleagues even thought that the guide on scenario planning I included in the original *The Art of the Long View* was giving away the store.

My theory was that we needed to grow the pie first. It was vitally important to make scenarios a standard component of strategic planning, simply because they help leaders make wiser and better decisions. Doing so would also position GBN as a premium provider of that service. (Today we would call this a "freemium" strategy). Not everyone agreed, but we decided to do it. And it worked. Scenario planning is an industry standard. GBN continues to be regarded as both a pioneer and an innovator in the field. And transferring, rather than hoarding, that capability strengthened our client relationships. Many of the clients we have trained come back to us for coaching, to facilitate especially difficult conversations about the future, and to develop and implement their scenario-based strategies.

The next thing we learned was not to make the course too dull, academic, or abstract. I remember our first course very well. It was held in our Emeryville office in 1990, before *The Art of the Long View* was published. The course was awful. It was effectively a three-day lecture which taught how to assemble a complex machine. There were many [overhead!] slides filled with bullet-pointed lists. Fortunately, a number of the people who took that course were both intrigued by the ideas and persistent and stayed with us beyond the first class.

It was my colleague Kees van der Heijden, another Shell alumnus, who figured out the best way to teach scenarios: make it hands-on training. He decided to do a mini-scenario exercise over a four-day course, using a hypothetical company with a particular strategic problem. And that's essentially how we still do it today. Each small group of participants chooses a willing "client" and then goes through the process of identifying the focal question, tapping external perspectives, determining driving forces and critical uncertainties, developing scenarios, and then presenting them to each other. While senior GBN scenarists provide expert guidance along the way, participation makes all the difference. Since what you're trying to teach is a skill, you're far better off doing it than talking about it. The course has been remarkably effective in spreading scenario planning skills far and wide. Vast numbers of people who have taken the course have been significantly affected by it, and continue to apply these skills in their work and their lives.

This ties into why *The Art of the Long View* continues to sell. It succeeds through simplicity. To do scenario planning well, there are better books—such as Kees van der Heijden's, *Scenarios: The Art of the Strategic Conversation*, which is a very good users' guide to the technique. It is comprehensive, rigorous, and rich with examples. But *The Art of the*

Long View is a particularly accessible introduction, which is why business professors recommend that their students read it to understand the idea and value of scenario planning.

We learned not to worry about giving away the store; generosity pays off. If you have a good idea or a tool, share it and you will be rewarded. That's what we found with scenario planning, which is a skill best taught in an interactive, hands-on manner — no matter whether you're teaching it in the classroom or the boardroom.

Black Swans and Asteroids

In 2007, Nassim Taleb published a highly influential book called *The Black Swan: The Impact of the Highly Improbable*. Taleb, who has since become a good friend, often says that the only answer to black swans is scenario planning — and that scenario creation is a function of good imagination.

What he means by a black swan is a highly consequential event that is almost impossible to predict. It is so rare that it seems to have no antecedents. The recent financial crisis, for example, would not be properly called a black swan. It was possible to see the antecedents and the plausibility of the scenario. We could have seen the evolution of the mortgage market and the abundant availability of capital, as well as the lack of regulation. We could have seen the scale of the shadow economy, if we had done our homework properly.

The eruption of Iceland's Eyjafjallajokull volcano in April 2010, which disrupted air travel all over Europe, was a black swan. As far as I know, no one had ever created a scenario of an Icelandic volcano producing such a massive eruption over a sustained period of time that it grounded this amount of air traffic. We know in principle that volcanoes can erupt, but we can't predict when they will erupt, or what the consequences will be. This requires an act of real imagination. We need to look around to see the sources of vulnerability might be, and imagine how they might play out.

A set of enormous and consequential events that really do require scenario thinking is asteroid collisions. These have happened many times in the past, but not much in recent human history. There was the Tunguska explosion over Siberia in 1907, but that was very modest in its impact because it happened over an uninhabited area and went unnoticed for a very long time. If that had happened over New York, there would have been no New York.

So this is a case where thinking about the potential black swans, and what might be done about them, can produce a useful response. Scenario thinking about asteroids helped lead to a movie, "Deep Impact," which I will discuss later. Apollo astronaut Rusty Schweickart, a long-time member of GBN's network, has recently devoted his time to bringing asteroid scenarios to the attention of world leaders. Rusty is chairman of an organization called the B612 Foundation, a collection of astronauts and scientists devoted to raising awareness of NEOs, or Near Earth Objects—the millions of tiny asteroids that have not been catalogued and could hit us at any time.

By focusing on this one particular black swan, and talking to as many heads of state, UN leaders, and members of Congress as he can, Rusty has achieved some real results. He has helped persuade NASA to undertake a survey of NEOs. He has called attention to a particular piece of space rock we already know about, one that has a slim chance of hitting Earth in 2036. And he has started to think about how we might deflect an asteroid (instead of trying to blast it out of the sky, a risky proposition that could easily backfire on us.) The Russian space agency has recently proposed a mission that would practice nudging an asteroid's orbit one or two crucial degrees in either direction, so that we know how to do it when the time comes (which of course it will, sooner or later).

Another black swan idea is geoengineering. This is where, if climate change gets too bad, we may consider taking drastic measures to reduce CO_2 in the atmosphere or reflect sunlight, such as seeding sulfur dioxide particles in jet trails in the upper atmosphere, or dropping iron filings in the ocean to create algae blooms that will suck down CO_2. Stewart Brand has begun work on several scenarios on how we might conduct these kinds of emergency measures, and the unintended consequences they might lead to.

Risky Business

Risk management is another arena where scenario planning can be a very significant tool. Risk management is the process by which organizations assess the magnitude and nature of risks that they face—usually financial risks, but also operational risks such as the breakdown of logistics or failure of suppliers.

What we have seen in the last few years is the failure of already flawed methods to calculate financial risk. When the subprime mortgage crisis erupted, for example, many companies that were deeply invested in securities had computer models designed to operate within a range of price dynamics from recent history. Typically, this history covered the previous 10 years—so the computer assumed that the kinds of changes in house prices before then were less likely to happen again. That leads to an extrapolative view of risk.

In fact, what we now know is that risks result from new combinations, new variables, new forces that make it very difficult to assess current risks in historical terms. The recent financial crisis is a perfect example of that. The risk management tools that many of the institutions were using did not reflect the scale of the shadow economy or its global interconnection. So the risks that people were taking were actually much larger than they knew. The instruments that had been created to deal with risk actually amplified the risks.

The remedy here is to use scenarios to think about entirely new kinds of forces. Not about what kinds of risks emerge from the model, but what kinds of risks would challenge the model. Scenarios force you to use multiple models of risk, not single models of risk. It's those single models that got institutions thinking they had accurately captured the nature of risk. The more you are required to have fundamentally different interpretations of the same reality — and take action on that — the safer your future will be.

GBN at the Movies

One of the most enjoyable developments at GBN in recent years has been the opportunity to contribute to a number of movies. Now, in hindsight, we can see the impact of films that tell stories based on future scenarios — such as "Minority Report," "Deep Impact," and the upcoming "Brave New World."

The first movie in this lineage came long before GBN was founded. It was called "WarGames" and was released in 1983. It's the first computer hacker movie and one of the first films where the nerd is the hero. In 2008, I attended the twenty-fifth anniversary version of "WarGames" — held not in Hollywood, but at Google's headquarters in Mountain View, California. Virtually every employee of Google was there, from founders Sergey Brin and Larry Page on down. It was clear that this film was a true inspiration for a great many of them. It came out when they were in elementary and high school, and was the first time they had seen themselves as heroes. Many of them knew every line from the film. Some brought laser discs of the original for the writers to sign.

Those writers, Walter Parkes and Larry Lasker, had approached me in the late '70s to help with an earlier version of the script. And the story they ended up telling had a good deal to say about scenario planning. The U.S. military sets up WOPR, a supercomputer with access to nuclear launch codes, after discovering in a training exercise that humans in silos are unlikely to push the button in a sudden launch scenario. WOPR's job is to run thousands of thermonuclear scenarios and "learn" how to "play" them better. Matthew Broderick's teenage hero changes this when he hacks into WOPR and is offered a choice of scenarios; thinking they are just harmless games, he chooses "global thermonuclear war." And ultimately the world is saved because the computer is forced to run through its scenario choices faster—and learns they are all futile.

The lesson couldn't be clearer—scenario planning (and risk assessment) is no work for machines. Human choice makes all the difference. (In his recent book *Cyber War*, counter-terrorism expert Richard Clarke claimed that the computer persuaded Broderick to play the game, whereas the reverse is actually true.)

Some years later, scriptwriters Walter Parkes and Larry Lasker joined GBN's network of remarkable people. And with a movie like that under their belts, it was only a matter of time before GBN became involved in their future screenplays. The next movie I helped Walter and Larry with was another hacker flick, "Sneakers" (1992), starring Robert Redford. This screenplay was built around a hacker scenario study done for the National Security Agency by the Stanford Research Institute when I worked there in the early 1980s. A scene near the end, where Ben Kingsley and Robert Redford discuss the role of information, money and encryption, came from what I wrote.

In the mid-1990s, Walter was tapped by Steven Spielberg to help create DreamWorks Entertainment—and that led indirectly to my involvement with the Spielberg-produced movie "Deep Impact" (1998). For this story of an asteroid collision, GBN worked with Spielberg to create a scenario of how the world would deal with inevitable doom. There were a number of elements of that came directly from our work, such as the way the government handled the crisis, the choosing of 800,000 lottery winners to join scientists and leaders in limestone caves in Missouri, right down to the use of an Orion rocket engine. My colleague, Eric Best, came up with the single most important contribution, I think—that it all came down to the question of whose hand you want to be holding at the end. And so the climactic scene where the heroine (Tea Leoni) clings to her father

(Maximillian Schell) in the face of a massive tsunami was informed, in a sense, from our ideas.

That was followed by our work on the film "Minority Report" (2002), also directed by Steven Spielberg and starring Tom Cruise. For this adaptation of a Philip K. Dick science-fiction tale, Spielberg wanted to make the film extremely realistic, and tapped us to help create the world of 2054. Our goal was to generate a set of iconic images that would become the references for this future.

Working with a team of about 15 people, we created many of the elements that were seen on screen: the urban form of Washington, D.C.; new modes of transportation (including cars that run up the sides of buildings), advertising, communication, and entertainment; moving newspapers, and the multi-touch computer interfaces Tom Cruise manipulates with special gloves. Having Spielberg realize those on screen was a remarkable privilege. The movie has since become a cultural touchstone, especially whenever multi-touch screens, personal advertising, or self-updating smart newspapers are discussed. Apart from a few silly details — if it were up to me, I would not have used those jetpacks — there's little I find unrealistic about the world the film presents.

Recently I was asked to help on the film of "Brave New World," produced by Leonardo DiCaprio and Ridley Scott, who managed to get the rights after a long period of negotiation with the estate of Aldous Huxley. Instead of making a historical artifact — that is, by reproducing every technology as Huxley wrote the book in 1932 — DiCaprio and Scott made the choice to update it. They asked me to help bring the book into the modern world. So over the Christmas vacation of 2009, that is what I did. I spent a lot of time reading the book. In many ways, it holds up remarkably well. Huxley was able to foresee a lot of our culture — Prozac, for example, is a kind of contemporary counterpart of Soma. But a lot of what we take for granted wasn't foreseen. There are no computers in the book. There's no space exploration. And there's very little in the way of modern biology (in 1932, we didn't even understand DNA).

The single biggest thing that I did in updating the book was to make it more biological. For "Minority Report," we deliberately left out a lot of possible bioengineering developments because they would have overwhelmed the story. I believe that the ability to manipulate biology is going to be among the greatest advances of humankind over the next century or so, and in this film we get to show a lot of that change. For example, the movie will feature buildings that are grown, energy that is derived from artificial bacteria, and the ability to enhance human beings. Bioengineering possibilities will be an important part of the subtext.

Perhaps as many as a million people have read *The Art of the Long View*, and maybe a few hundred thousand have come across other things I have written. But many millions of people saw (and will see) these films. So the ability to embed scenarios in these kinds of films is a very powerful tool, and I look forward to seeing what else we can do with the medium.

DRIVING FORCES

In the original edition of *The Art of the Long View* I wrote a chapter about the global teenager, which I identified as a new "driving force" in the world. At the time we were seeing something new among young people—a great deal of global mobility. New modes of telecommunications were increasingly available. In those days we weren't really talking about the Internet or even mobile phones. The most advanced technology teenagers had their hands on were VCRs.

What we wanted to know, as I said in the book, was "what will be the interplay between this new global adolescent community and the evolution of the new electronic media?" GBN sent one young colleague around the world to interact with his peers in 17 countries, which led to this prescient insight: "New communications technologies are becoming so powerful and so cheap that teenagers all over the world will be able to afford them," I wrote. "The global teenager will want to communicate this way, and using these kinds of new media tends to change people's behavior and values." Looking back from the era of Facebook, smartphones, and YouTube, it's hard not to say that we got this basically right. If you had invested in a portfolio of teenager-friendly technologies 20 years ago, you would likely be extremely rich now.

So what unstoppable global forces will drive the next stage of the twenty-first century? My answer to that can be summed up in one big (and unfortunately, rather gloomy) idea: the systemic crisis. This is all about our complexity and interconnection, which serves us so well in so many ways, ultimately leading to a crisis of crises.

A whole set of factors have come together to create the systemic crisis. First, there's *interconnection*. More and more systems are connected internally and externally. More and more things affect more and more other things. We send a constant stream of information, goods, and people from one place to another. My situation is a good example. I operate on a global scale that was simply not possible before. The level of airline travel and telecommunications we have now didn't exist even a few decades ago. Financial systems are interconnected in ways that have never existed before, as are telecom systems, pipelines, energy systems, and global logistics. And these systems are connected to each other in ways that aren't always obvious. For example, finance and global logistics are closely related. High-speed logistics on a global scale require a tremendous amount of financial liquidity and lubrication. Our extremely sophisticated IT systems let entire industries hook up for mutual benefit.

A good example of all this is the global flower market in Aalsmeer in the Netherlands. This is a facility where cut flowers from all over the world are brought every single morning to be auctioned off and flown back out to countries all over the planet. Not only does it depend on jumbo jets, but also computers and telecommunications. Watching the shipments as they come in via the Internet, the wholesale flower buyers instantly bid and set prices. This setup makes the fresh-cut flower business possible on a global scale by offering an unprecedented level of physical and virtual interconnection. If any one part of the system broke down, the global flower market would come apart—and indeed, that began to happen when the Icelandic volcano grounded air traffic in Europe. (Markets that transport fruit and vegetables from Africa to Europe were even worse off.)

The second factor here is sheer size or *scale*. All of these systems now operate on a much, much larger scale than before. We're getting larger agglomerations of institutions. Some are companies with huge reach and market caps—global giants like Toyota and Google and IBM and DuPont. Some are new agglomerations of nations: NAFTA, China and its sphere of influence, India, the expanding European Union, and an emerging Brazil.

We're seeing economies of scale in nearly every industry. We can build things of a size that we never could before, such as the Burj Khalifa skyscraper in Dubai, the tallest tower in the world at nearly 3,000 feet, which opened in 2010. Records are being broken in nearly every industry. Take the Airbus A380, now the world's largest passenger aircraft, or the Three Gorges Dam in China, already the world's largest electricity generating plant though it won't be fully operational until 2012. Even scientific instruments are breaking records, such as the Large Hadron Collider, the world's largest particle accelerator. We have financial resources on an unprecedented scale, in the hands of individuals and institutions as well as governments. Global GDP has hit a tremendous $60 trillion, while global debt is almost four times that at $220 trillion.

The third factor is *speed*. Our information systems move at the speed of light, so we can interconnect electronically at a speed we never imagined. Computer trading, global logistics, and mobile communications are perpetual. We are always connected, always available, always on. We rarely get to walk away from a project, even when the work week ends. Smartphones put the ability to work at all times in our pockets, and that creates entirely new kinds of pressures.

The fourth factor is *diversity*. This system is hardly homogenous. It contains many different kinds of actors. Even in the supposedly monolithic public sector, diversity is rampant. We have states, cities, countries, and regions pitted against each other. The economic conflict between Greece and Germany within the European Union is but one recent example. The U.S. is very different from China, India, Brazil, Russia, and so on, and each one of those countries has tremendous internal diversity. The same is true of companies and industries, NGOs and non-profits.

When these four factors come together, the result is the fifth factor: *complexity*. Complexity means that the link between cause and effect is not simple. In a simple system, if I pull a lever, I get the expected result. If I turn my wheel, the car turns. In a more complex system, I turn the wheel and there may be a very large amount of lag time. I may get what I want, or the result may be something completely different. Systems have become too complex for anyone to manage or even to understand. Earth's climate is a great example of this, and we are effectively producing more systems that are a lot like the climate. Small changes now can produce very large-scale changes downstream.

When humans attempt to respond to problems within these complex systems, we get the sixth factor: *incoherence*. The recent financial crisis is a perfect example. We saw an incredibly interconnected financial system, a shadow economy on a massive scale, events that were happening with tremendous speed, and many actors within the system with different views on how to fix it. Yet the complexity was so great that no one understood exactly what effect a fix would have. So the response was fairly incoherent. It was more proactive than the response we saw from governments in the 1930s, at least, but not as good as it could have been. In part, that was due to a substantial difference in interests at all levels—between Democrats and Republicans, between the U.S. and China, and so on. Each had different views on how to deal with the crisis, and all dealt with in their own ways. There was no significant coordinated international response.

That's the seventh and final facet of the systemic crisis: it is *out of control*. No one is in charge. That doesn't mean that individual actors can't nudge and influence the system. We all influence the system in significant ways. But no one actor dominates the stage. There was a period during the 1990s when the United States was genuinely a preeminent power, but that time has passed. The U.S. is not in charge, China is not in charge, and Europe is not in charge.

Some degree of hierarchical restructuring will be necessary to establish order at a high level. This is what we have seen in biological development, human development, and societal development. One part of this restructuring will involve the network of institutions and laws set up in the wake of World War II, such as the UN, the IMF, and the World Bank. Another part will be informal: a reorganization of relationships between nations, marketplaces, societies, and networks of individuals. But it is clear that this system still needs to achieve much higher levels of coherence, some degree of control, and the ability to guide itself.

So what does this all add up to? It means the complexity and scale of potential problems are so great that the systems we have put in place to deal with them may not be up to the challenge. As a result, whether it's climate change, financial crises, or global terrorism, it is entirely plausible that we may be overwhelmed by the magnitude and nature of these crises. That's what I mean by a systemic crisis.

This is not new; the idea of the systemic crisis has been around since the late 1960s, and rose to prominence during the 1970s via books such as *The Limits to Growth*, commissioned by the think tank The Club of Rome in 1972. In 1977, I wrote a series of studies for the President's science office on the inability of large-scale complex systems to manage themselves. The prevailing view by the late 1970s was that they were not up to the challenges we were facing. A series of failed presidencies were used as evidence: Kennedy was assassinated; Johnson didn't run again because of the Vietnam War; Nixon was driven out in disgrace; Ford was a caretaker; and Carter was overwhelmed by the energy crisis and America's malaise.

The 1980s saw one kind of response to the era of complexity. President Reagan had a very simple view of reality and a very clear set of priorities. He sliced through the Gordian knot and restored a sense of presidential power. America began a wave of extended growth and prosperity. This was a period where the issues and challenges were fairly modest, wars were infrequent, the economy was doing well, and the Soviet Union collapsed. There was some degree of hierarchal restructuring. The modern European Union emerged out of that era, as did NAFTA. And it turned out that some of our systems were more resilient than we had thought. For example, we adapted to higher energy prices rather quickly. People bought more fuel-efficient cars, started using public transit in greater numbers, and employed a number of technologies to save energy at home and in the workplace. The price of oil plummeted in part due to these changes.

So the notion of systemic crisis vanished from the intellectual agenda for a couple of decades. Now it has returned with a vengeance. In one important way, the threat level is lower: we no longer have to contend with the possibility of sudden accidental nuclear war between two global superpowers. But in many other ways, the risk of systems spinning out of control is much greater. Is history repeating itself? Are we going through a tough patch, as we did in the 1970s, from which we'll come out stronger on the other side?

To answer that question, we'll have to see how the world deals with the evolution from a resource economy to a knowledge economy. This has been underway for quite a while, as technological power has grown and as our dependence on access to physical resources has diminished as a source of economic value. The need to move tons of ore or agricultural commodities and the limits of seasonal cycles set the pace of the old world. Then, for a while, you needed to be technologically capable and have abundant resources as well. The U.S. was the extreme example of success built on both resources and knowledge.

To understand why this is no longer the case, look at Singapore and Nigeria. Here are two countries that became independent at around the same time: Nigeria in 1960 and Singapore in 1965. Since then, their fates have been radically different. Nigeria, with abundant resources such as oil and natural gas, has made almost no progress. Singapore, with no resources at all, lifted its people from poverty to relative wealth in a single generation. It demonstrated an ability to build economic value on the basis of skill, knowledge, and capability.

Good government helped, but it also took a population that was able to lift itself up by its own bootstraps. Singapore made a substantial investment in mandatory education, and spent a lot on higher education too, sending its students to some of the world's best universities worldwide. Singaporeans became increasingly sophisticated, educated, and capable. This is only possible where economic value derives principally from knowledge. That same phenomenon happened in Japan, Korea, and Taiwan. We are now seeing it play out in China and India.

The greatest value in the world today comes from knowledge — the ability to reinvent how we do old things as well as to invent entirely new things. It is being much more effective at manufacturing or distribution or logistics — or at entirely new tasks. Take the search engine industry, which barely existed 15 years ago. Now it is one of the great sources of economic value in the world, a market worth more than $22 billion. The last decade has also seen a boom in national search engines — in Arabic, Hindi, French and so on.

That's the knowledge economy: reinventing the physical economy as well as doing new things entirely outside the realm of the physical. So the institutions of knowledge are critically important: universities, venture capital, and all the other forces that contribute to turning knowledge into economic value. Some places are particularly good at getting knowledge, but not great at turning it into economic value. The U.K. is famous for this. Jet engines, radar, and DNA were all discovered in Britain in the last century, but commercialized in the U.S. Growth, no matter where you are in the world, is a matter of expanding the frontiers of knowledge and then embodying that expansion in economic value.

The expansion of the knowledge economy drives many of the forces behind the systemic crisis: interconnection, scale, speed, and complexity. The imperative of this economy is accessing, distributing, and exploiting information. The speed of information matters, even when it isn't true. Rumors spread instantaneously on the Internet and can produce riots around the world in days — for example, the backlash against anti-Mohammed cartoons published in a Danish newspaper in 2005 that led to attacks on Danish embassies. In May 2010, we saw how a computer error drove the U.S. stock market down 1,000 points in a matter of minutes. The SEC put "circuit breakers" in place in a bid to prevent this from happening again, but traders are always smart enough to find away around regulatory limits. Circuit breakers are unlikely to prevent future systemic stock market crises.

Another important variable in this tale of the systemic crisis is the rise of China. So far this century, China has been the greatest success story to emerge from the world of autocratic capitalism. That means capitalism that is state-driven, pragmatic, and non-ideological, but where the power resides very much in the center. Singapore was a good example of that, but China became an even better example. The challenge for China is that it is becoming extremely complex. The autocrats at the center must deal with the problems of a society where you have about 400 million people who have already climbed out of poverty, and another half a billion who are desperate to join them. So it's not a small challenge.

Meanwhile, there is the question of whether the U.S. will ever recover its dominant role. There are a large number of experts, on both the left and the right, who suggest America is in permanent decline. I believe the U.S. is fundamentally dynamic and will come back. Its entrepreneurial culture is still unparalleled. The financial system is willing to take risks on new ideas. And it still attracts the best and hardest working of the world's immigrants.

But if the U.S. does fade relative to China's emergence in the world, it will make a great difference to the shape of events. Think of the first half of the twentieth century, when the U.S. came into its own and Britain faded. If the U.S. recovers while China powers on, then we have a systemic crisis of two rivals with very different visions of the world and different visions of the rules of the game. The third possibility is that they could both be overwhelmed by systemic crisis, since the U.S. and China face many of the same kinds of issues. China can mount a centrally driven response to problems like climate change, whereas the U.S. clearly cannot. America's democracy is essentially gridlocked, making it extremely difficult for us to respond to many imminent challenges.

Another key question is the role of international institutions. These have provided stability, structure, and order since the end of World War II. But China is not accustomed to playing within or building such institutions. Does this mean we are going to return to the world before World War

II, shaped mainly by alliances and state interests? The U.S. has generally been committed to a world of law and institutions. Will it remain so? President Obama is committed, but it is not at all clear that the rest of the country—or his successors—will follow his lead. What we have is an extreme crisis of global governance, which may not have the self-organizing quality of a market or the top-down organizing power of a government. We may have a system out of control, in other words.

The final piece of the puzzle is Europe. It is becoming clear that the continent was not ready to launch a single currency, the Euro, because of the magnitude of the difference between rich countries like Germany and poor countries like Greece. They now face a seemingly intractable crisis of internal diversity, which threatens to tear the Euro apart. The EU seems as deadlocked as the U.S. political system. If Europe uses all of its bandwidth to deal with internal crises, it can't be an effective partner for the United States in the global game with emerging powers such as China, India, and Brazil. That's just in economic terms. In military terms, much of the continent has lost the will and the means to fight, Britain being the exception.

The disasters that could result, which we'll explore in the following scenarios, are not at all hard to imagine. They include the potential for various kinds of cyber warfare, abrupt climate change and major natural disasters, internal and trans-border wars, financial crises, nuclear and other WMD terror, even pandemics and plagues. They are particularly important now because there are simply more people in the areas that would be hardest hit. All of this adds up to a massive problem that could strike in the years immediately ahead. Indeed, we may look back and say that the systemic crisis was already well underway by 2011.

SCENARIOS FOR 2025

This chapter focuses on the scenarios themselves. We will reflect on the scenarios that took us from 1990 to 2005, then make a STEEP analysis of the global landscape over the next 15 years. (STEEP stands for Social, Technological, Environmental, Economic, and Political forces.) Finally, we will look ahead 15 years into the future with three scenarios for the year 2025.

Looking Backwards: The 1990 Scenarios

Let's begin with a reflection on the three scenarios I wrote for *The Art of the Long View.* How insightful were they? And how useful would they have been if you had them in your hands 15 years ago? My sense is that two of them were actually pretty good. The *Market World* scenario captured the spirit, dynamics, and many specific elements of the world of the 1990s, in particular the rising role of business and the evolution of the Internet, including the transformation of commerce that came with it. It saw a relatively peaceful, stable expansion in the post-Cold War world. That scenario worked very well as a description of the near-term future.

The *Change without Progress* scenario was a good description of the 2000s. It had elements of terrorism, financial crises, conflicts, and disruption. There were some gains, but not enough for people to feel a real sense of progress, particularly in the wealthier parts of the world. But it would've been quite perceptive about the last decade.

Of the three scenarios, *New Empires* was the most off-target. This was a scenario built around protectionism, trade blocks, and competition between those trade blocks. It was very much a scenario of the moment. There was a lot of discussion around the beginning of the 1990s when Japan was on the rise and Europe was coming back. MIT economist and author Lester Thurow said that the U.S. was going to be defeated by powerful competitors from Asia and Europe. Unless we organized trade blocks, Thurow argued, we were going to be too weak. This scenario was built around his logic. It would've almost been impossible not to have that scenario among the set, since it was such a dominant line of thought. But it just didn't play out that way at all. We didn't see trade blocks developing beyond the European Union, which was as much a political entity as an economic one. NAFTA did not turn out to be much of either.

It is possible that *New Empires* is still in our future. Perhaps competition between China and the U.S. will lead in that direction. But I doubt it. The nature of the competition has changed in fundamental ways. Ultimately, the *New Empires* scenario shows the weakness of being trapped by the perceptions of the moment.

How useful were the scenarios as a set? Very useful, I think, particularly because *Market World* would have enabled you to see the information technology, network-driven boom of the 1990s. Early on, you would have recognized many of the signs of change. You would have seen the meaning of the World Wide Web becoming widely accessible and the evolution of companies such as Amazon, Apple, eBay, and Google.

Similarly, you would have recognized the politically fractious environment of the 2000s as a sudden turn into *Change without Progress*. A lot of the features of that landscape would have been evident. The rise of terrorism, conflict in the Middle East, and economic downturn could all be seen at the beginning of the decade. We knew that wealth was concentrated in the hands of a relative few, and that there would be minimal progress for the middle class. You would have had a good guide to strategy in a world that was very different from the previous decade, in both spirit and substance. You would also have recognized fairly quickly that *New Empires* had become history, not the future. So as a set, the 2005 scenarios didn't turn out so badly.

Step by STEEP

Now let's look ahead. I often find it useful to think about possible futures by creating a STEEP framework. To reiterate, that involves examining a combination of social, technological, environmental, economic and political factors and forces.

SOCIAL FACTORS

There are three social dynamics I want to touch on. The first is the continuing rise of religion. Religion has become a more powerful force in the last 20 years and is likely to become even more so in the decades ahead, particularly in China and Africa. What we are going to see is Christianity and Islam on the march: Christianity in China, and Islam and Christianity in Africa. Already in Nigeria we have seen a small-scale conflict becoming larger because of religious tensions between Muslims and Christians. The dividing line runs across central Africa, and could easily become a new focus of disruption. It also could become a major driving force in China. Singapore, one of the best-managed Chinese societies on earth, is overwhelmingly conservative Christian. That seems to have helped the country focus on education, meritocracy, and hard work — the classic Protestant work ethic. Now imagine what China might be like as it becomes relatively conservative Christian in its orientation over the next few decades.

The second social dynamic is the challenge to white rule. For the last four centuries, white men have dominated the world. European colonialism was followed by America's military and economic dominance of the planet, and both Europe and the U.S. were predominately and culturally white. That world is vanishing fast, and it will continue to vanish. Not only are native peoples unwilling to be dominated by foreign cultures, but Europe and the U.S. are facing waves of non-white immigration. Middle Eastern, South Asian, and African immigrants are drawn to Europe just as Hispanic and Asian immigrants are to the U.S. California, Florida, and Texas are typical of the demographics of the future.

What we're likely to see in more and more places in the U.S. is non-white economic and political leadership. The day when whites will constitute a minority of Americans is not far off. The clearest indicator was the fact that Barack Obama carried every group except white males, the old power guard, in the 2008 Presidential election. In Europe, the tension between the new non-white, non-Christian immigrants and the old, white Christian order is profound and growing.

The third social factor is the rising power of women. Particularly in the wealthy world, more and more lawyers graduating from law school and more and more doctors graduating from medical school are women. In the U.S., women are already the majority of graduates in both of these occupations (as well as the majority of college graduates overall). What does this imply? As in the past, the establishment of the future is likely to be dominated by lawyers and, in many instances, by doctors. If you go into healthcare, you end up near the top of society in a variety of ways. So what we're likely to see is women exerting more and more political and economic power. In a few places and in a few times, the female factor may become extremely consequential — especially in the Middle East.

TECHNOLOGY FACTORS

There are so many areas of technological innovation and growth that surveying their potential future is a book in itself. I'll limit myself to discussing seven of the most promising new technologies.

1. Smart Networks. Over the next few decades, networks will become ubiquitous and cleverer. The iPad and tools like it will provide access to information anytime, anywhere in a great variety of forms. These networks will be very smart, not only in the sense of tracking you and knowing what you want to do, but also in knowing what you need before you do — enabling smarter cars, a smarter flow of goods and finances, and a much smarter flow of information. The deepening of networks around the world, with embedded intelligence, memory, capability, and software, will become increasingly powerful.

2. Augmented Reality. We will have a variety of devices that will enable us to gather information about where we are. Walking down the street, we will be able to see the contents of shops, or menus from nearby restaurants, or directions in front of us. We may be wearing some kind of lightweight augmented reality glasses, or we may have the equivalent of our iPhone or iPad seeing in front of us. Many Android and iPhone apps already have this functionality. This can easily veer into the kind of fantasy realities sci-fi author Vernor Vinge described in *Rainbow's End* (2006). Imagine running around the streets of a city playing augmented reality games. When you look at one of your friends, for example, you may see a mythical creature rather than a human being. Imagine a kind of live-action version of *World of Warcraft* and you're getting close. We'll see this technology in the business world too. Imagine an augmented reality meeting where you literally see notes on the people around the conference table—their names, titles, specialties, and what you really think of them.

3. Synthetic Biology. One of the fundamental scientific revolutions of our time is the ability to modify organisms, particularly microorganisms. We are now able to modify the essence of a bacterium, effectively programming its behavior. An E. coli bacterium has been modified to produce an anti-malaria drug called artemisinin. In May 2010, genome scientist Craig Venter unveiled the world's first synthetic bacteria, its DNA constructed from component chemicals. Soon Brazil will see its first large-scale production of bacterially produced ethanol. The bacteria consume sugar cane and produce ethanol. This is the first of what promises to be many products that use biological processes, which will require much less energy and fewer resources. We can expect a great variety of fibers and plastics made this way. Almost anything that has an organic molecule at its core will be vulnerable to this form of production. New super strong biological materials could take the place of steel and ceramics. Fairly complex products could be produced biologically. One might even imagine organic circuits—and organic computers. We'll also see synthetic biology in the medical world. It is very likely over the next 15 years that we will witness an enormous improvement in treatments for a great variety of diseases, as well as for many of the infirmities of aging.

4. Energy from Bacteria. Synthetic biology leads us directly to a new energy economy. By 2030, large volumes of hydrocarbon fuels — methane, gasoline and diesel fuel — will be produced directly from bacteria. We will, in effect, have a limitless supply of hydrocarbons, supplanting our need for fossil fuels. Best of all, the bacteria require carbon dioxide from the air in order to grow, so the whole process of creating and burning the fuel will be carbon neutral.

5. Small Scale Nuclear. Burning fuel to produce electricity is still a dirty process, even if the hydrocarbons come from bacteria. Pollution issues will still lead us toward non-hydrocarbon fuels, particularly small-scale nuclear power plants. We'll see technology like pebble bed reactors or Gen IV nuclear power plants that can burn nuclear fuel without producing plutonium. (Stewart Brand covers this area extensively in his book *Whole Earth Discipline*). These plants, small and safe enough for local communities, will use what are in effect nuclear batteries. You don't take waste out. You simply bury the battery after a few decades of use. This waste will be stored temporarily for the next 50 to 100 years — while we develop better battery recycling technology.

6. Super Macro- and Micro-Manufacturing. Large-scale, high-volume, low-cost production is about to take off. So is small-scale manufacturing — stuff built by devices that resemble today's primitive 3-D printers. This will give us the ability to make devices at home. By 2030, the idea of making your own smartphone will not seem unusual. You download the software, insert your materials cartridge, wait a few hours, and out comes your new phone. This means highly distributed manufacturing. Artisans will use this process to produce custom-made objects in a great variety of styles. (It won't be too much of a threat to manufacturing industries, since most of us will still prefer the hassle-free route of buying products from the nearest big-box store.)

7. Water Technology. No matter what, access to clean water will be one of the world's most urgent issues over the next few decades. Technology will be developed to clean existing water, capture water, and desalinate water. We're going to see more and more places doing what Singapore does today — that is, capture a great deal of rainfall, reprocess all its industrial and commercial wastewater, and do a great deal of desalinization. This is possible today, if pricey. The technological challenge is in making these processes less energy intensive.

ENVIRONMENTAL FACTORS

Unfortunately, the twenty-first century is certain to see many new, challenging sources of pollution. The expansion of electronics, solar power, batteries, new chemicals, new molecules, new pharmaceuticals, new kinds of pesticides will provide many benefits, but also generate new forms of waste. Given the scale of the global economy and the expansion of manufacturing all over the world, this waste is likely to be distributed far and wide.

On the other hand, as the world gets richer, what we'll see is more and more places getting cleaner. This is already starting to happen in Europe, the U.S., and Japan. In 2008, I was struck by Beijing's effectiveness in dealing with pollution for the Olympics. They set targets for air quality — a tough job in Beijing, as any visitor knows — and achieved them. What we're going to observe is a cycle of pollution. As wealth spreads, pollution will increase, but then diminish as we employ more and more clean technologies. Cleaning up is going to be big business.

The big uncertainty is climate change. Clearly, today there is not enough global willingness to deal effectively with climate change. European countries are willing to move more radically. The U.S. and China are far slower to act. And there is uncertainty about what is likely to happen. If climate change begins to happen fairly abruptly, that may accelerate the rate of response. But if the science remain uncertain and the effects more distant, the response is likely to be very small and limited in most parts of the world.

ECONOMIC FACTORS

Here the big question is whether the world will return to relatively high levels of productivity. I think the answer, on balance, is yes. The fastest-growing parts of the world are likely to become much more productive over time. China, India, and some of Latin America and Africa, all areas that were highly unproductive in the past, will get new production methods, new organizational models, new levels of integration, and ultimately much greater productivity. Just as we got more sophisticated in our economy in the rich world, they are likely to do so as well.

The greatest area of economic uncertainty is globalization. How effective and continuous will it be? If we continue to see globalization spread, we'll get a more integrated and richer world. If it breaks down, that will diminish the absolute increase in wealth. The global knowledge economy is dominant, but it may falter—because of constraints on intellectual property, say, or a breakdown in education, or diminishing levels of mobility, or other constraints on the movement of knowledge. Meanwhile, if the cost of access to resources becomes greater, thanks to climate change and water shortages, we could see the balance of power shift back toward the resource economies and away from the knowledge economies. The Middle East, Central Asia, Africa, and the western part of South America could all gain from this.

On the whole, most countries have gotten the message about the importance of education. But will education spread and grow around the world? Will the quality of education improve? Will we see higher education in more and more places? If the answer is yes, we get more productivity. If the answer is no, we get more social distress and conflict.

There's one last set of economic questions. Who wins? Who wins among countries? Who wins among classes? How does the growing pie get sliced up? Do we see widespread growth around the world with more countries (and more middle classes) getting to play? Or will we continue to see wealth concentrated in a relatively few countries or in a global upper class? Over the last decade, we saw a disproportioned share of the growth in the U.S.

going to financial companies. That's one of the reasons the middle class didn't advance, and why growth was relatively weak. It was trading profits, not investment profits. Trading does not yield high growth directly. It only yields growth if those traders invest in growing companies and other productive assets instead of luxury goods, mansions, and yachts.

POLITICAL FACTORS

The first political question we must ask is one that has been around forever. Who will have power, and what kind of power will it be? The uncertainties around the nature of political power in the U.S., China and Europe are great. Europe is struggling with the challenges of governing a diverse group of nations. Britain elected its first coalition government in 60 years. The U.S. is deeply divided and facing enormous challenges from countries like China.

The final political conundrum is the nature of the systemic crisis I described. We will inevitably go through a degree of systemic evolution. Will we see a self-organizing, bottom-up kind of new order? Will we see, as historian Niall Ferguson argued in the journal *Foreign Affairs*, a world of increasing anarchy and disorder? Or will we see some form of order imposed from the top down, coming from a variety of sources?

THREE SCENARIOS FOR 2025

Now, let's look at three plausible scenarios that flow from these driving forces. All three are built around the fundamental question of how the world could deal with the systemic crisis looking forward from today in late 2010.

1. CASCADING CRISES

The first scenario is the darkest of the three. In many ways, it's an extension of the last decade. What we discover is this: that 9/11, the tsunami, the genocide in Darfur, and the fall of Lehman Brothers were just the beginning. Society's systems failed to adequately cope with those crises, and they continue to fail. Individual countries, businesses, and NGOs are unable to agree or to act effectively. Even when they do agree, their capacity to act is limited. The scale and complexity of the crises seem beyond our human abilities to manage. Goodwill, when it emerges, is inadequate for dealing with the magnitude of the crises. There's even disagreement about the nature and the cause of these crises.

A good example of that is climate change. Despite a scientific consensus, there is, sadly, still no agreement among the populations of the world on what climate change is, if it's actually happening, its causes, if and how it can be changed, who bears the responsibility, and so on. Most leaders get it, but the electorates as a whole don't. (Recent U.S. and U.K. opinion polls found movement towards the ignorance end of the scale.)

In *Cascading Crises*, this kind of systems language problem becomes typical, and all intractable problems connect to each other. So climate change leads to massive water shortages, which causes problems with food production, which leads to mass migration, which produces a whole range of political and economic troubles.

Looking ahead from 2010, I can imagine a number of events that can trigger a cascading crisis. It might begin, for example, with Iran. As the mullahs come close to actually carrying out a nuclear test, the West might find it necessary to invade. That would lead to a widening Middle East crisis, an insurgency that stretches from Iraq through Iran, Afghanistan, and Pakistan. You can imagine growing conflict in Saudi Arabia and Yemen, a succession crisis in Egypt, widening wars around Israel in Lebanon and Syria, another Palestinian intifada, and unrest in Sudan, Ethiopia, and Somalia.

How are these countries drawn into the conflict? Well, what I'm really talking about is a kind of "war zone" that extends in both time and space stretching back to the first Gulf War and all the way into the future. It is governed by one unchanging narrative — that the U.S. is at war with Islam.

This is an agreed-upon fiction pushed by political extremists on both sides. It takes places in countries that are in very deep trouble, and have large groups of fundamentalists challenging somewhat more pro-Western regimes. Afghanistan and Iraq are only the latest examples of this.

This is a war fought in the minds of millions of individuals, each one of whom can make a devastating difference. We saw a perfect example in the recent guilty plea of the Times Square bomber, Faisal Shahzad. An American Muslim, Shahzad was profoundly affected by what he perceived to be reality—that the United States was out to kill Muslims.

So you end up with a zone of low-level conflict that reaches from the Indian border in Kashmir all the way around to Somalia and Ethiopia in Africa. American and European troops are involved in this zone for a very long time. They have to keep the oil flowing. There is no way forward and no way out. This is less like World War I or World War II than the permanent extension of a decade when the United States fought three wars at the same time: Iraq, Afghanistan, and the war on terror.

Another area that blows up is the Korean Peninsula. North Korea starts it, by sinking a South Korean ship. Things are getting particularly weird in North Korea. It is not hard to imagine a variety of unpleasant scenarios that disrupt the success of South Korea and occupy the political energies of Japan, Korea, China, and Russia—all neighbors trying to confront what could be a crazy state in North Korea.

One could easily imagine Nigeria imploding over oil and religion and culture and tribalism. This is a country that was previously dominated by Christians; now it's split between Christians and Muslims. And these breakdowns also fall pretty heavily along tribal lines.

We see water crises in Southeast Asia, as access to the Mekong and Irrawaddy Deltas becomes vital. There is growing international conflict in South America as left-wing and right-wing regimes fight it out, with Brazil caught in the middle. Grudges that go back to the age of Cortez explode into new rivalries. An aging leadership in Venezuela gets ever feistier and fights it out with Colombia. With its oil wealth, Venezuela is able to fund conflict around the world. Mexico becomes a widening mess, largely driven by the drug wars.

Even the great engine of China begins to slow down as it is driven by its own internal stresses and inability to manage systemic issues. Like previous colonial powers, China finds itself dragged into conflict in Central Asia, Africa, and perhaps even Korea and Vietnam. How would China justify this adventurism? Very simply: China still sees itself as the Middle Kingdom, the civilization at the center of the world. It has a sense of fundamental superiority. Who better to police the planet in its most troubled times than the most civilized nation?

Disease hits China in a major way, brought back by their African Expeditionary Forces. This has as great an effect on the Far East as Spanish Flu did in Europe in 1918. Perhaps it is a new strain of tuberculosis, resistant to antibiotics. China ends up quarantined. Even so, the disease reaches Korea and Russia, becoming a major outbreak with millions of deaths.

In this kind of fractious environment, you would see a lot of covert protectionism. Very little of it would be acknowledged publicly. But there will be lots of efforts to protect local jobs, local industry, and local wealth. In this world, multilateralism is dead. To the extent that deals exist, they are one on one.

Crime is on the rise in this world, cybercrime especially. We see increasingly common disruptions of information systems and financial systems. The force my colleague Nils Gilman calls "deviant globalization"—the massive global black market for everything from weapons to drugs—turns itself into a kind of invisible nation, one with a very strong, utterly unregulated economy.

Terrorism is on the rise. War is big business. We see the beginnings of biologically-enhanced warriors in this scenario. That means everything from giving soldiers drugs to speed up their thinking to fitting them with implants for improved vision and hearing. Limbs could be replaced with superior prosthetics.

Religious and ethnic conflict becomes ubiquitous, whether it is rivalry in the former Yugoslavia or Christians fighting it out with Muslims in Africa. We see the challenge to white rule everywhere. European and American civilization is being challenged wherever it can be, including at home in the U.S. and in Europe where non-white groups rise to challenge the dominance of the white Christians in their own countries.

You might even see a small nuke being used in this scenario, perhaps to take out the American base in Dhahran, as well as Saudi Aramco's oil facilities there. It might be a stolen Pakistani nuke delivered by a Yemeni Al-Qaeda.

This leads to a rush away from the dollar. Oil is no longer priced in dollars. But there's no alternative currency, so we see money rushing all over the place. There's a dramatic fall in international liquidity. Gold becomes the international reserve currency of desperation, hitting $3,000 or $4,000 an ounce. Economic growth and trade are highly volatile. Recoveries are short-lived. Incomes are not rising. This is the world of global anarchy that Niall Ferguson wrote about. By 2025, you would see a few wealthy islands in a sea of poverty, with lots of new sources of pollution. The world is in many ways one big environmental disaster.

So that's the really dark scenario. It takes the trends of the recent past into a world where the system is fundamentally unable to cope. Consider this an extrapolation of the Bush era, or a continuation of the *Change without Progress* scenario.

2. THE GREAT EAST-WEST MATCH

In this scenario, the world is fundamentally shaped by the rivalry between the United States and China. Both countries succeed, but neither can dominate. The U.S. has to work very hard to match China's size. China has to work very hard to match America's head start in technology and wealth. But both are doing reasonably well. The U.S. makes significant economic progress, and takes the competitive challenge seriously. China is able to lift 500 million people out of poverty. They become effective rivals.

This is a scenario of competitive progress, but not one that is particularly stable or friendly. It is peaceful but not comfortable, because both nations are attempting to align the world in their favor. As in the Cold War, the important spheres of influence are Africa, the Middle East, Central Asia, Southeast Asia, and South America.

At its root, this is a rivalry between democratic capitalism and autocratic capitalism. Does the Anglo-American mode of democracy and capitalism really yield rapid progress? Does it have the ability to adapt fast? Or will it be bettered by the economically driven, scientifically thoughtful version that Singapore pioneered, and that Korea, Taiwan, and Japan also pursued?

Which direction India takes is one of the great questions in this scenario. It too is wrapped up in the global ideological competition between the American way and the Chinese way. Europe is still internally focused, dealing with its issues of immigration, currency, and how to deal with the impoverished corners of Eastern and Southern Europe. It doesn't play a very important role in this great rivalry.

This is not the clash of civilizations envisaged by author Samuel Huntington. It's more the rivalry of civilizations. China and the U.S. are not really against each other. Their economies are far more interdependent than those of the U.S. and the Soviet Union ever were. The rivalry more closely resembles the earlier relationship between the U.S., Germany, and Japan. There was often friction between those economies; indeed, the collapse of the gold standard in 1971 was a function of their rivalry.

We see a new space race with China playing the role of the Soviet Union and the United States reprising its role. Europe and India might also take on China in space, with NASA taking a back seat. (In 2010, both Indian and Chinese space programs already have designs on Moon landings.) But if the U.S. really decides to get into the game again, there are many directions in which a space race could go. We might find ourselves in a race to get back to the Moon, or to Mars, or to stake our claim to mineral-rich asteroids.

We also might see the U.S. and China squabbling over Africa and South America. Today, China is very active in Africa, but the Africans don't love them. The U.S. has largely ignored Africa in favor of markets in Latin America, but South Americans resist being dominated by the U.S. (or by anybody else, for that matter). If the U.S. starts to get involved in markets in Africa as an alternative to China, the Chinese might get more involved in markets in Latin America as an alternative to those gringos in North America.

By 2025, you would see a world that was better off, with poverty steadily shrinking even as the political conflicts and tensions in the world continue to rise. In effect, this is a return to the *New Empires* scenario. That idea couldn't have been further from the truth in 2005. But perhaps it was 20 years ahead of its time.

3. LONG BOOM II

This is the most hopeful scenario, where the world sees a return to the boom times of the 1990s. It is congruent with the *Market World* scenario, as well as my book *The Long Boom*, in which I saw growth potential for the next 20 to 30 years. The fundamentals of the twenty-first century global economy were always strong—driven by consistent growth in technology and enterprise. They were simply obscured by brief recessions and what turned out to be unfounded fears of terrorism.

This is a scenario driven by productivity, innovation, and globalization. We see entrepreneurs inventing entirely new industries and reinventing old ones. This leads to a sustained increase in productivity in the United States, China, India, Russia, even Europe, as well as growth in Latin America and even in Africa. It is a world of increasing coherence and self-organization. Using smart information systems and highly distributed networks, institutions are able to begin to deal with the scale of global problems, whether finance or trade or commerce or climate change. There are new modes of organization that build from the bottom up, not the top down, enabling increasing competition and collaboration at the same time.

The global marketplace is lightly but effectively regulated. As a result, there are more winners than losers. A true global middle class begins to emerge. A knowledge-driven economy spreads rapidly around the world. Wikipedia, it turned out, was the model of the future. Access to knowledge, built from the bottom up, distributed well, and used effectively on a global basis, becomes the driving force of economic development.

In this scenario, we deal indirectly with climate change in the name of efficiency and security. We become much more energy efficient, we make our own power, and we become much less dependent on energy resources distributed around the world. Most energy is produced locally using bio-technologies, small-scale nuclear power plants, and renewable energy. Less oil and gas is moved around the world. Coal technology becomes practically extinct.

We repair and upgrade some of our most workable and flexible international institutions, such as the World Bank, IMF, and World Trade Organization. Some contentious institutions, such as the UN's Security Council, are replaced with more sensible and universal mechanisms. The rule of law prevails. Environmental regulation and Internet regulation happen at a global scale.

This new cooperation and competition plays out most effectively in Africa. The world is finally able to provide the security that enables development in that once-troubled continent. What one gets, in effect, is an international police force establishing order in Africa, ending the cycle of military coups and disorder. Development and education finally take off.

The greatest surprise of all happens in the Middle East. The area finally begins to modernize as the result of a political revolution driven by women. Spurred on by the martyrdom of Neda Agha-Soltan in Tehran during the riots of 2009, the women of the Middle East finally challenge the men. The police can't open fire on their wives and their daughters when they march in the street en masse. Their demands: equal rights, an end to the burqa, better education and healthcare for their children, and better maternal care. It is a major challenge to the misrule of Islamic men in the Middle East. It succeeds and drives an explosion of openness, cultural change, and productivity in the Middle East.

This is a world where both India and China also take off. Russia develops a modern and relatively benign autocracy (call it a tough-guy society). Private space flight accelerates. There is no space race between nations; on the contrary, we see tremendous cooperation between a reinvigorated NASA and the European, Russian and Japanese space agencies. The next space race is between billionaires to get to the trillions of dollars of mineral wealth in the asteroids.

So by 2025, we have a booming global society with vastly more people well off than poor. And best of all, the prospects for our global future look great as well.

* * * * *

Of course, we don't know which scenario will come closest to unfolding. In all likelihood, the future will hold elements of each. But if there is one thing I have learned repeatedly in the past 20-plus years, it is this: The world may be uncertain and unpredictable but that's no excuse for being unprepared. We have more access than ever to the data knowledge, ideas, and tools that we need to shape a better future for us all. ▪

ACKNOWLEDGEMENTS

Special thanks to Chris Taylor, my writing partner; to my editor Nancy Murphy; and to the dedicated "Planet Schwartz" team of Christine Haker, Vanda Marlow, and David Babington. I am deeply grateful to my fellow cofounders, without whom neither GBN nor this book would have been possible: Stewart Brand, Jay Ogilvy, Lawrence Wilkinson, and especially Napier Collyns, who remembered every anecdote and corrected more than a few. Thanks also to GBN President Andrew Blau and all of my GBN and Monitor colleagues — past, present and future — and as always, to my wife, Cathleen, and son, Ben, for their enduring love and support.

Made in the USA
San Bernardino, CA
29 September 2017